McGREGOR SCHOOL

. . . AND OTHER POEMS

Also by the Author:
Airling . . . And Other Poems

McGREGOR
SCHOOL

And Other Poems.

by

Gerald Clarke

THE GOLDEN QUILL PRESS
Publishers

Francestown   New Hampshire

Library of Congress Catalog Card Number 80-65158

ISBN 0-8233-0310-1

Printed in the United States of America

In memory of
Douglas McGregor, 1906 - 1964,
from whose writing I learned most
of what I know about human enterprise.

CONTENTS

Part I

Part II

PART I

McGREGOR SCHOOL

1

McGregor School was David Stark extended.
He was a captain patterned on the sea
across whose changing, changeless depths
he moved and found his meaning.
Season followed season, the moon
marched through its cycles, shifting winds
blew permutations and the teaching crew
who manned the school
were altered with each passage:
no two
among the children who grew up
crossing and recrossing
as they sailed and learned from sailing
had voyages alike.
Briny, cool and coursing
like the surf off Pemaquid,
Stark matched the sea in all respects save one;
like all men, he was mortal.

David understood
the storm lashed fury of the surf,
the harsh sheer mass
of unexpected ice
and rocky promontories in the night
and yet he chose to sail. He knew
how other captains managed, how
they disciplined their crews, but he

explored uncertain straits, with his
stout crew he sought
sure harbors on a still uncharted coast.

He sailed with this conviction — sailors love
the sea, and mates and cabin boys
have stakes in every voyage, so
that weathering a storm
and making landfall at some harbor goal
counts more than wages earned
to working crews. Stark kept
no heavy irons in his hold, no whips
to force his will. He gave himself
unstinting to the mission of the ship
and found the crew
would match his vigilance and care
and bring the craft, true seamen, through all straits
till quiet seas were found.

The children learned from this, for they
were passengers and purpose for these trips,
these crossings which left magic in their wake:
McGregor School.

2

"No, Bill, I think you're wrong," Dave said,
"a teacher's task is limitless,
it has no end, it's infinite."
He pointed to the *ojo* on his wall,
an Indian design, a good luck charm
contrived of sticks and yarn.
"That 'eye of god'
might be a symbol of our calling,
a warm caduceus for teachers,
a never-sleeping eye
that watches over children
night and day."
        "O David, please!"
from Robin in alarm.
        "You know me well
enough," said Dave, "to know that I'm aware
how frail we are, how short
our seasons run. But Bill says
wear it like a smock, this teaching role,
and hang it in the classroom when you leave."

"Don't we deserve," defended Bill,
"to be ourselves, to make our own mistakes?
I give my teaching everything I've got
while I'm at school but after hours
I wear no special cloth, I have no vows
to keep."
        "No vows?" persisted Dave,
"I think that we have promises to keep.

When I was young
I thought that it was reading that I taught,
but now I know
it's children that we touch,
beauty we defend against the beast —
the line is thin
between the cultivated field
and the wild insistent press
of jungle closing in.
Physicians, teachers, those
who work with people have
a calling constant as the cry
of life for help."

"Medicine
is something else again," insisted Bill.
"With death the adversary there's no doubt,
but sleepless eyes for teachers? — no,
I can't see being at the beck and call
of kids who need me little if at all."

"Well I remember," Robin ventured with
a smile, "a cycling trip I took with Dave
one summer day a while ago, when I
would gladly have foregone that sleepless eye.
Two raffish lads went by along the wrong
side of the road. Dave spoke to them, and not
at all unkindly, of the rule, and one
of them gave him the single-fingered ges-
ture of contempt. Now I would say forget
it, let it be, but David turned and cut

those two lads off and chewed them out, — some words
about respect for age and listening to
advice. I saw their anger blaze, their quick
resentment of Dave's trap, — then wonderment
took over, some small sign they might have learned
before they went their way.
Well I was worried then. Still if I had
to choose, I'd hold with Dave
that teaching's what I am
not what I do."

Children at the school —
their faces in the corridors of time
like shadows and swift colors, racing
over summer's rolling, patterned hills.
I see them
the children of today and yesterday,
their lives beautiful
and fragile as
bright blossoms in the spring.

Faces of children at the school — the future,
the present, and the past.
Is this a window or a mirror on the wall?
Who is that who stares so steadfast
back at me and moves to speak
and then is gone?
Who are they,
our children or ourselves
somehow grown young again?
Who made them what they are,
these children,
the children at the school?

4

"Thank you, Barbara, for giving me
a chance to share this past month with your class,
for they have entered on
the last adventure of the human mind
left after infancy and speech.
To learn to read! To grasp
these six-and-twenty characters we use
to enter, to record our every thought
and nuance!"

"David, we
appreciate your part in all of this,
for you illumine with your love
of language these first steps. I know,
I've taught a lot of classes, never one
like this with you assisting. They
have caught something from you —
I've seen it many times these past few days
when time stands still for them,
a hawk in an updraft
motionless
in some precarious balance
before it plummets on its prey."

"I know, so swiftly they move on,
they read and then they write,
they mimic then invent.
A few short years and one of these,
the neophytes, will write

17

as Tammy in the fourth grade did
a day or two ago,
'Cats' paws
have secret pockets
for their claws.' "

Time began
one day in early May.
Rain fell within the courtyard
of the school. Oblivious and safely walled
from all that might intrude we played,
a timber wolf and I.
His role — ambassador
for all endangered species
of the world, to teach the young to care,
and I a pilgrim looking for a bridge
my fathers crossed too many years ago.

Foregoing lunch, enisled
with ancient strength and beauty, cleansed
by rain, I talked to him;
my voice seemed no offense
and gravely he attended.
Then, having heard
the music of the wolves, I howled.
My canid comrade listened for a while
then, lifting his great muzzle to the sky,
he joined the joyous music that I made
and he accepted me.

                Rain falls
again. This is no August day.
It is the ninety-third of May.

6

From the highway to the east
as Stark approached the town at night,
the low clouds caught its glow.

"Adam," he mused, "I see your face,
it hovers like a disembodied ghost —
your lonely face blown giant, nothing else —
in that patch of light above the distant town.
Why did your father leave, how could he sire
and then abandon you? I find it hard to understand
creators without conscience
breaking patterns, breaking lives.
Adam, your name is legion
in this town today, you children of
the abdicated fathers, reared
by mothers left alone,
by working mothers trying to fulfill
too many roles, apartment dwellers,
lost ones, with their lovers for a season,
their emptiness,
their broken dreams and you.

How warm and constant as the sun
I still recall
my own dear father. He was always there.
But where have all the fathers gone
in this town and the others, how
can I be surrogate for you,
forgotten sons
abandoned by your fathers?"

I hear the song these young men sing:
What's a kid or two to me?
I'd like to see him through,
the little guy,
but growing takes so long and I can't wait.
I've got myself to think of, what the hell.
Oh sure, my father hung in there
but that's a different story, he
had nowhere else to go.

If you look back it seemed ok
to have a kid. It didn't work.
It's no one's fault, but he'll make out
somehow. I'll do my part,
take him a day or two each week
and share support. Better we make the break
than stick it out and hassle all
the time. What kinda deal is that
for raising kids?

Why is the earth
so fecund at some seasons? Cottonwood
is white across the lawns as summer snow
and maple wings are strewn too lavishly
this year. It frightens me, this gross excess
of life, it leads to dreadful dreams
of lemmings moving seaward in a wave.

I call you "son", Terry,
I hold you close,
rejected consequence
of adolescent coupling.

But it's too little and too late.
My love and all the care
that your adoptive parents give to you
cannot offset
those first three years —
a child berserk,
blown rootless as a tumbleweed
by every prairie wind.

I give more love and constant care
each week of winter to the birds
I feed than you received
your first three years of life.

9

I pass him in the hall,
carrying I think some secret tune
inside himself, some march
to which he moves,
and I hear violins and cellos,
tubas, clarinets,
initial squeaks and bellows
mellowing until they speak
a language I'm denied.
I feel a need
for other throats and other tongues than mine
and seated in the darkened concert hall,
I thank the music man
for gifts that he has given them,
the children of the school.

This melody has moved me
to distant places, other races —
wolves howling and a rising gibbous moon
in the wilderness on Isle Royale,
their tribal music lovely past belief.

10

Peter, on a Sunday afternoon
I pause before your sketches on the wall,
standing out like asters
against the common grasses of the field.
A boy of ten, yet you evoke
old dreams, forgotten themes — your art
now teases like a half-remembered word
I summon up in vain.

Awake o journeyman hunter
the tigress where she sleeps.
Far off is the sleeping village
where other men rest this night.
For beauty is fraught with peril,
a tigress with fang and claw,
magnificent, treacherous, playful,
hot eyes and whimsical maw.

11

Claudia. A housekey, daily
on a green ribbon
around your neck — it seems
a symbol
of a childhood that never was.

I see a generation of children
like you, without parents
till after five,
walking home with keys
to open heavy doors
on silent rooms
eerie and foreboding.

One afternoon in April you came home
to find your father dead, and you alone
for two long hours
without a mother, priest or friend,
silent on some stark and alien shore
with your amulet,
your housekey on a ribbon round your neck.

The news is full of ghosts this week.
Children at the school from years gone by,
their faces half-forgotten, suddenly
in one brief week attain
a local prominence; the journals run their names
and photographs and reading, I remember
times gone by.

I remember Barbara,
a child so bent on self-destruction
nothing could deter her.
Winter winds are blowing
and the news is full of ghosts this week —
I half expected this, the story on page one —
the sequel to the symptoms
no one, it seems, could stem.
We met you at eleven, Barbara,
and I remember your parents with no thoughts
but their concerns, but others have survived
as bad. I never understood
why you became a child alcoholic,
a thief, a nameless, faceless dialer in the night,
schemer, and worker of mischief past belief.
And I remember now that raw December day
three years ago, when I dismissed the buses,
saw them off, and saw
among five hundred children going home,
raw hatred etched on every line
of your young face — of me, your father,

those young and nameless bees
already buzzing
around your presence and your promise —
you hated all of us.

A freezing rain today,
the ice-bound branches make
tree travel treacherous for squirrels
and the roads
no place for youth and hurried indecision.

13

(Robin: Transcript of a conference tape).

Only here and now and for
a little while to come these things
are true about your child. We cannot say
what ten years more will bring, or whether she
will find success in college, that's too far
away. You say she started reading to
her dolls at four; her progress here these past
two years is quite in tune with that. She needs
some help with number facts, some exercise
to build her speed and confidence, I'll send
a set of cards to work with and some games.

But tell me more
about her stamp collection, would she like
to show it to the class some afternoon?
I know, she's shy and unpredictable.
Encourage her at home, I think
she's nearly ready now.

14

Stabbed your teacher with your pencil:
treed in the jungle gym,
a cornered animal at bay,
you curse authority with baleful eye.

Twin brothers one year older,
and left alone by parents who believed
that children need no meddling by adults
to settle their own feuds.
Somehow you survived.

Benjie, this day was difficult: it leaves
another window open in the wall
between us. A year ago I could not bear
even to let the wind blow on your wounds
still left from infancy. Today
you have survived a winter gale.

15

"I don't approve," said Mrs. Thomas Kent,
"of outdoor education. My Gina like to froze
last week with Mrs. Framingham, off tramping
through the woods in February — that's
not what school is for."

                    "Not all a school
is for," smiled David in reply. "This was
a voluntary thing, a recess extra, not
required, and Gina spent this Monday afternoon
researching and reporting on the birds
she saw that day."

                    "She's happy as a clam,
she loves her teacher, those two are just alike.
That girl has got no sense, but I'm her mom,
I say it makes no sense to walk the woods
in winter, why should teachers put such nonsense
in their heads? Let's have some useful facts
in school, why fiddle with the birds?"

"Why walk the woods? Yes, why would anyone
stand motionless an hour or more
in a snow packed lane
among the stark and dormant trees
with arm outstretched, his numbed
hand mittenless and filled with seed,
except to hear a sudden whir of wings
and feel a body light as eiderdown

30

perch sudden on his finger?
We walk alone and alien on this earth.
A child is fortunate
whose hand remembers tiny perching feet
and trusting feathers warming what they touch."

16

He comes, a bearded Nemesis,
if that disguise can be, rotund,
with an eye like a Viking whaler
searching for oil.
And once having fixed his harpoon
in the flank of a certain prey
he follows, relentless, impassive,
the same shadow fleet in the depths.

When Iver Lundgren, chairman of the board,
stomps in in his whaling boots
he's not seeking information
but obeisance, the respect due his age.

He courses about the school's waters
one quick inspection trip;
a thousand images beat against his eyes,
he chooses six to scorn.

Bewildering. Year after year
wherever Stark goes, wherever he leads his school,
the shadow of Iver Lundgren
occludes the sun's warming rays.

The tented class slept through the summer night.
On early morning watch,
Stark stirred the embers of the fire.
Bill Meyers watched
and sipped his chocolate.

"Dave, how should teachers teach?
You've seen me these two weeks
do things I've never done before
and I feel good
yet I don't know.
Out here in August in the woods
the school I've always known seems far away,
old ways, the blackboard and the chalk — out here
we haven't used the usual books
and yet they've learned,
I've seen them grow,
I've watched them write and write
in strange new ways."

"There are a thousand ways
to teach and learn, but means
determine ends. The question is
what kind of people do we want
to follow us when we are done
with leading and determining the path
we take? The young will learn from us,
harangue them how we will,
because the mind
the quick electric mind

strikes fire from every storm that blows
and rubs some essence from each passing cloud
and patterns it and knows."

"I think you're right. I'd like to see
this camp idea grow, perhaps
embrace all children in the school
another year, not just the few
on trial here. You shake your head?"

"A paradox. It's Washington,
not Auburn, funds this camp. I can
persuade a distant bureaucrat
to fund experiments like this,
I lack the guile
to sell it to the parents of these kids
as something more than summer fun.
We swim against the currents of our time
and outdoor education won't survive."

Unbelievable
that love would build a cage,
bricks to keep the household safe from harm,
bars to thwart a hated world of change.

Phyllis, plain of face,
denying fashion in your homely dress,
barred from college,
never free to travel,
prisoner of your parents' morbid fear —
stroke the somber chambers of your cello.
That minor melody
foretells the night, the bridge,
the desperate jump,
the end of all you might have been
with their acceptance.

Phyllis, child in chains,
in agony I see
the sterile steel arches of the new Bay Bridge.
There'll be no place to hide
in all that winter night for you,
a wretched parricide.

(School board meeting).

David, advocate of children,
sits helpless while his plans are lost at sea,
and he the sailor knowing every wind
can never touch the tiller
by their rules.

"O it was bad," he later told his friends,
"that crew, the Board of Education, lubbers all,
debated half the night,
lips luffing and the children's needs becalmed.
For hours the sails flapped endlessly
in strong but unproductive winds,
no seaman there to trim them,
set the course toward landfall
and move in."

"Ruth, how is Karen doing?"

"Not so well.
She has her lucid days, but often she's
alone and wretched in her little shell.
I'd hoped she'd open up, but there's a thing,
a darkness, Dave, that I can't dissipate."

"How does it show?"

"Most days she has these fears
and sometimes she just curdles up with hate
against her father. You would not believe
the tales she tells, poor troubled child — she makes
the other children actors in a play
that always has the same dark theme, she takes
the role of victim of their devious plots,
peoples the world with demons and with gods,
attributes motives, cunningly contrives
to save her life in spite of fearful odds
which simply don't exist. You think her home
accounts for much of this?"

"Her father hates
her, I'm afraid. He tries to do
his duty as a father but he broods
about her birth, his wife's long illness. He's
at once a victim and an agent of
distress. The climate's bad. He blames the child
for all her mother's grief. So Karen's all
unfit for human love — suspicious, wild
and out of touch with people."

"David, she
imagines more mischief in a morning than
I've met in thirty years!"
                              "I know it, Ruth.
You have no hope?"
                              "David, she's alive!
She's only twelve. There's always hope. Just see
her running now among those sunlit trees!
But, David, you look weary."
                              "I've not slept
since four this morning, thinking of this child,
wondering if we can meet her needs . . . "

"O Dave, you must be dead and it's not right
for you to father all these kids through all
their childhood ills."
                              "I really didn't mind
it, Ruth, one sleepless night, oh no —
else would I not have heard
the oriole so pensively
articulate his matins, coloring gold
those first grey hours
before the sun
stood truly in the east
and day was here."

38

I saw the pride in your father's eye,
how tall he stood as he held your hand
while the nurse injected adrenalin.
The swelling drained
from your half-closed eyes
and breathing came easy again.

Carlos, gentle Charlie,
allergic friend of a drowning bee
in a rain-filled pool,
your heart will do you in,
tu corazón, amigo.

I think I know as I see you two,
the source of your warm compassion,
and better the pain by ungrateful bees inflicted
than life abandoned by a heart constricted.

Crayoned pictures
of the way you see yourselves
deck the kindergarten walls.
True primitives,
your stark stick figures march
against no backgrounds
or huge heads mounted on two feet
tell all the tale.
Black and green, lilac, yellow, red —
what might the colors mean?
And here's a family of four
with ears not represented,
but belly-button circles
centered in each oblong body,
and there a tortured scribble
from which two solitary eyes
survey with wonder
some black cubistic structures.

Crayoned pictures
on the kindergarten walls —
barely out of infancy,
man the dreamer
with his bright recording eye
with his deft responsive hand
puts the world he knows on paper
shares his song with other singers
stores his memories in books
climbs the lonely path of knowing.

The buses roll. The guidance team convenes:
the home-school counselor, the nurse, a pair
of classroom teachers talking with the coach,
psychologist, speech therapist, and Tom
O'Brien, resource teacher for the school —
they meet with David Stark. Around and round
the comments go. Some eighty years expe-
rience and fifty years of study sit
around that table, one small boy the fo-
cus of their thoughts. He is not there, but he'd
be stunned if he could know how much
they cared.

      Sean, fearful Sean,
the victim of a gargoyle who appears
when you're alone and in the dark of night
to threaten that you'll die when you're fourteen —
you used to think that these were nightmares,
now they seem more real.
Something touches you, but nothing's there,
and other children laugh to hear you talk
of voices, apparitions, fearful things.

"Such visions are not rare," reports Bill Dell,
"although to most of you, Sean's problem must
seem strange, indeed. The answer seems to lie
in giving reassurance, talking out
the fears Sean has, and finding ways
to give support. You're doing that, I know."

"Well, I've good news," says Susan Hunderup,
"I talked to Mr. Reilly yesterday
and he agrees to try Tom's Labrador
suggestion."

    "Labrador?" Bill asks,
and Tom says, "Yes. You see, last week I had
Sean out to my home for an overnight.
We have three Labradors, the one a pup
named Lucky. Lucky never left Sean's side
the whole week-end, it was a mutual thing.
I offered him to Sean if his parents would
agree, a friend, you know, a comrade and
a guard."

    "It just might be the thing," smiles Dave.
"A man and dog together are a pair
to face the terror and the darkness of
the night."

    "I told him," Tom concludes, "to love
this dog, to care for him, to play and talk
with him, to learn to listen when he speaks,
sleep with him always in his room, and trust
his ears, his nose, his loyalty to him."

5:10. It seems the middle of the night
in the long dark tunnel of December. Now
nine cars roll on their separate ways. No mir-
acles, no final answers but
a plan of action and some hope.

24

You dash through
the crystal corridors of your mind,
bewildered, never knowing
which Richard is you.

A pair of walking psychopaths,
your parents never should have met.
Bright, suspicious of the world,
they flee ceaselessly from rules;
you hamper them.

Gone without a trace.
We might have helped, we came close
to knowing you. There will be
sharp splinters
fatal shards when you leap out
to flee the crystal prison of your birth.

A tabby in first heat,
you prowl the April streets at ten o'clock,
meowing invitations
to disaster.

You begged us not to tell
your parents, not to seek their counsel,
you said that teachers talk with kids
and teachers understand, but your old man
would beat the living hell out of you,
and you were right — you paid.

The jungle is no place
to find what you are seeking, Toni.
Rejected, clawed from groin to shoulder,
years from now a solitary cat
will lick its wounds and growl.

26

The curtain fell. The audience
applauded. Lights came up. The play
was over. Freddy, only six,
caught David's hand. "Was that
the play?" he asked and looked
quite hopefully around. Just down
the hall stood Philip Sanibel,
enthralled. "Oh that was wonderful,"
he cried, his eyes still glowing from
the magic on the stage. "Oh, thank
you, Dr. Stark, for giving us
this morning. Wow!" "You're welcome, Phil,"
Dave laughed. "It was our friends, I think,
in fifth and sixth, and Mrs. Wright
in music, made the morning for us all,
and I enjoyed it, too." He clapped
his young friend on the shoulder, sent
him off.
            With Sarah Wright and tea
that afternoon he shared the day.

"Two kinds of people," Sally mused,
"the Freddies and the Phils — the ones
who never get enough, who stand
up from a feast with hand outstretched,
and those who never see a star
between two clouds without a song
of gratitude for beauty glimpsed."

I knew your father, Paul,
he conned me for
three thousand dollars, seven years ago.
A flim-flam man, whose silver tongue
could build an enterprise
whose day was always
just around the corner from tomorrow.

I think that I'd forgiven him till now,
till I heard you explain away your role
in Jerry Thorne's misfortune. Oh, I know
that each of us is born unique, and yet
how quick we mimic, unaware we pick
a pattern for behavior from the world
that's close and hard about us from the start.

Those promises! Those long-forgotten lies —
"the father's sins . . . "

Who's lying to me now?
— not Paul, I think,
but Caldwell's next of kin.

"Preposterous, sheer fiddle-faddle,"
stormed Iver Lundgren,
chairman of the Board,
"this plan of Stark's which mixes lunch
with recreation at that school.
McGregor School has come to be
a country club, a place to play.
Those children should be learning how
to work, to buckle down and do
a job. It's loose as a goose around
that school. We need some changes there."

"You miss the point,"
responded Tom Mastrotto, "my two kids
are learning faster than they ever did
before, and if they love their school, why what
is childhood for?"
                    The Board soon turned
to other heavy matters for that night.

But Lundgren will not lose
an argument so he begins
to plan for he will have
his moment on the stage,
however long delayed.
He hates to see another garner praise
he covets for himself and David Stark
is all that he aspired to be in life,
a leader with a quick command of words —
but swift, too swift with repartee.

Iver says
he doesn't care what people think
but oh, he does, he scans the village press
for letters which applaud him.
When hostile lines appear
he seeks redress, adroitly finds
some crony to support him,
come next issue.
He works long hours at nothing else
than building up an image for the world,
his little world, the one that counts,
to notice and admire.

"D'you think we'll have a fire drill today?"
Mark asks, and clutches at my sleeve.
Timid Mark, wee mousekin of a boy,
no reassurance I can give
can quite erase
the anxious lines from your fear-twisted face.

Born premature
and sheltered by your worried parents since
from every hazard
in these seven years of life — I still recall
how over their objections
you moved on
from first grade to the second.
You bring to mind
how maple leaves in August sniff the chill
and, taking fright, assume October's reds
before the frost comes truly on the hill
to send the chipmunks shivering to their beds.

"Leaving, Robin?"
           "Soon. I still have time
to talk with you, come in. O Dave, I'm bushed,
this day has been too long."
           "For me as well,
but this is light. I liked your reading group
this morning, liked especially the way
that Jill has just caught fire. Last fall she seemed
so lost, so woebegone."
           "And all your thing,
dear David, your suggestions — she
reminds me of
an inchoate verse,
the first few strokes
of pen on paper when
you're still not sure
how the song will go,
but sing she surely will."

"I'm glad. You think that she'll survive the stress,
her broken world, her broken home, this rift
that cleaves her down the middle?"
           "She has found
herself, she'll be alright. I've been this route
with Teddy as you know,
and they survive, yes, somehow they survive
and Jill will, too . . . You're still not sure?"
           "O it's
not that, but seeing you just now so like
the month of June, dear Robin, and myself

50

well past the equinox I try to say,
'Just let the years pass by
and be content. You're not a god:
enjoy autumnal things, the sweet
clear voice of children and the warmth
of fire on cool November nights,
go chat with neighbors, talk of soil
and prospects for an early spring.
This is the age of astronauts,
an alien world, its poetry
a cybernetic program.' Yet
so many times, dear friend, dear one,
I've needed
to have my head pressed warmly to your breast
a little while
a little isle of peace
to have the child within me comforted.
Instead there is a multitude
of people and of problems
a babel of shrill voices
an orange void and in its heart
grotesquely grinning frogs
mocking shattered dreams,
and I too gravely gentle
too old protective strong
to tell you this."

"I know it, Dave. I think I understand.
Somehow it never happened. We meet
in public places almost always. God knows
there have been others. But you
are special, Dave. I've needed you

as counselor and comforter, as someone
to believe in all these years — needed you
as no one else, as friend or father,
fellow creature, there is no category
for what I feel for you, and seeing you
about the school, so Christ-like
in your patience . . . "
                              "Robin!"
"I'm sorry, Dave, for you are human first
of all, but somehow proud, too,
and self-sufficient as a cat —
I've rarely felt you needed me
or anyone — you give so patiently
so freely of yourself that I have guessed
you have some secret source
where you renew yourself."
                              "I'll never tell!
Cat-like? Yes, there's a chord
that I respond to. But even cats,
you know, for all their chosen
loneliness, at their own times
and seasons, for curious
and arcane feline reasons
need quiet times of human love.
It's getting late."
                              "It's always late
in busy lives like ours. A kiss
before I have to go? . . .
Good-night, dear Dave."
                              "Good-night."

January, and the snow too cold
for packing. Angel wing designs were traced
in every quarter of the noon-hour field.
David Stark pulled on his boots and paced
out toward the area where Kathryn Bates,
his colleague whom he'd come out to relieve,
was scribing rhyming words across the snow.

"Such diligence! It leads me to believe
you people'd rather read and write and spell
than race with me out to the swings and ba⁀k,"
and led the laughing group a merry chase
that ended at the bus loop cul-de-sac.

"How is your daughter, Kate?"
                              "Oh, Dave, she's at
that magic age, she's three, you know. Last night
she saw the crescent moon, a first for her.
'The moon is broken,' she called out — a phrase
to make me think of other broken moons —
I guess the pictures in her story books
show full moons only. Every day for her
brings some discovery. She touches, looks
and hears with such a sense of wonder. It's
a magic age and too soon gone. I learn
from her and teach my nine-year-olds some ways
to find out what they're too old to discern."

(Enchantment - the art room).

He held them in his hand at five o'clock,
the residue, the art room's nightly treasure,
reminders of the lessons taught that day
caught golden in the pale November sun.

He half remembered bits
of tinted yarn that he had known
in childhood, scraps
of texture, lint
the wind drove in his eyes
or lodged to warm
some secret crevice in himself.

Perhaps, he wondered,
a child's day
is like a piece of string
caught up and woven
with a thousand other strands,
idiosyncratic, random, caught
unlike and isolate
from any pattern known.

Russell, Howard, Mark —
you are indeed
your father's sons.
Even at seven and eight and nine,
that taut and rigid stance
repeats a pattern known
too well to me. It shouts
male arrogance, proclaims
your porcine lack of feeling.

The court assigned your mother custody
but how can she
communicate with you? — a woman, one
who talks each morning with the birds
she feeds and cries
when she finds feathers scattered on the ground.

Be engineers, my lads,
and work in steel and stone.
The one kindness you can do
is not to touch
a dog or horse or woman
made of flesh.

Turn the tube and watch
the patterns change, so swift
geometry can alter and
the myriad colors shift —

then look out there,
the playground, with your clear
but retrospective eye.
And who are these
who whirl around
the merry-go-round
and jump their ropes so gaily
or wheel their infant sons and daughters
along the sidewalks daily?

No longer you and I,
so short the spring
and summer and so swiftly
autumn's come.

A lifetime ago — I was just nine then —
the flight of a flicker from a summer field
startled me. I can see it today
as clearly as then. I can't forget
the bird and the day and the least detail,
and a special meaning it had for me
at nine and a little past.

And Rachel, I
remember the day you came to our school,
a writer, a dreamer, a weaver of tales,
with one small window
in your inward eye
through which you dared not look.
So write me a tale of a small, scared child
and give her a name from your secret store;
then tell me why, in this story of yours,
this little girl runs so lonely, so lost,
and cries when it rains in the fall.

(Last day of school).

Goodbye. Good luck. The sun
stands still, my heart's at solstice too
though I've seen summers come
and summers go and autumn come
at length. I should be season-wise
by now and yet I see
more endings than beginnings here,
and lads and lasses who
no more will run to me
at midday for a hug, a secret
shared or check to see
what tie-tack I have worn today.
The vintner knows each autumn brings its grapes
but nothing quite like last year's purple capes.

I think that it's the spirit of these times,
not destiny, that moves me through
these changes — why
so sudden under bright September's sun
should I abandon my career
and crawl into the chrysalis of change?
This is not early death
to leave my work to younger men to do
and I still strong
and master of my trade.
I've seen so many changes that I look
with wonder more than fear at these strait strands
I weave about myself. I still have dreams,
new life emergent from the grey cocoon,
and these sustain me through a waning moon.

PART II

CASCADE

A yellowed torrent, a
cascade of autumn leaves
assails the ground. No wind
impels them, bitter cold
last night has cut them down.

The cowbirds peck bewildered
at altered water hard as stone
in their familiar bath.

Leaves drop as though the trees
could carry them no longer,
as though the ground were avid
for each one to fall, to touch,
to rest and rise no more.

This day is terminal.
A squirrel scurries after
fallen nuts and I

alone of all who walk
these woods remember how
these trees bore summer like
a green enduring force
so short a time.

Expectant now they stretch
stripped limbs against the sky.
Those stalwart trees
are fortunate — there'll be
no other spring, no second May for me.

SCARRED TREE IN THE FOREST

I see it standing there,
a scarred and ruined tree
ready for my axe.
I'll bear it like a fallen comrade
log by sectioned log
to warm my hearth this winter.

I think in years to come
the storms will strike me as they struck this tree,
the crackling affinity
of wind-brushed clouds
for outstretched limbs,
too many winds will snap too many boughs
my leaves desert me
and the sap run dry.

I may remember as I stand
defiant of that last
and too destructive torrent
of electrons from the sky —

this day
the way
the sunlight darted through your hair
the words we spoke
the softness of your breast and lips
the love and joy we felt —

thinking to myself that I may be
firewood on your hearth
in afteryears.

64

LADY IN BLUE

We were not intimate — I never knew
whether she slept in a shirt or a gown
or nothing at all — but she was one of few
who spoke my native language. She could find
the word I needed, accents lost
until she came.

I dreamed of her before we ever met,
a lady robed in blue,
dark, slender and soft spoken,
her words like music uttered in a tongue
I understood but could not speak,
some language from a common past we shared.

Incarcerated inland
this sailor listens for
the language that he knew in youth,
remembered syllables,
the sounds of surf on shore.

NOT AS LITIGANTS

Let us not meet as litigants
across some paneled room,
the tedious words so deadly, cold
and circumscribed by precedent.
Deep frozen in old tomes, they inch
like glaciers from the foothills of
the past to crush and petrify
all future hot contenders caught like us.

We need no barristers
to lead us step by step
through courtly minuets
to reach a resolution under law.

I think if we should battle through the night
with no attendants, none to referee,
the outcome might be more acceptable
than verdicts from the bench and twice removed.

FANTASY

I could believe
here on this night bound beach
with its brine still salt on my skin,
the waters dark with kelp
warm brown and somehow vital,
that this is a sea of blood
insistent on the shore.
Is there not
a littoral like this,
primal, passionate,
incarnadine and sleepless
somewhere inside some recess
of my mind? What else
should summon me and why
does the hot heart shout,
"Mother, embrace your son,
I hear you, know
you, and I come!"?

ABENDLICHE HÄUSER

A boy lived in these houses years ago
on Buffalo's east side,
two story rentals, tiny tended lots,
and he came back years later
to find himself —
an attic where he used to play,
a window where his cat would come and go
on nightly prowls.

            He'd thought
a city aged more slowly than a man,
but here was one
turned ruin overnight.
All in a gathering darkness and decay
the houses stood where they had stood before,
their windows broken, boarded up,
no children in the streets.

The man remembered rooms where he had slept
from Spain to Amsterdam,
rebuilt and firm against decay
and standing where they stood
when towns were walled.
Which is the old world, which the new?,
he mused.

MARCH REPRIEVE

Today I woke
to hear the chirring of the red-wing
just returned — bright "whick-er-dee!"
across the late-thawed fields —
so strident, brash and clear.
It held a promise that
the unused wood,
stacked birch and maple
kindling sticks and sectioned logs,
accrued in last fall's expectation
of harsher winds and deeper snows
than winter brought this year,
will have another summer's seasoning in the shed
before this blackbird flies,
and I shall have
a summer of reprieve
before he leaves.

SUNDANCE - A WOLF FRIEND

You might have come from outer space,
so rare a visitor,
your kindred numbered in mere thousands
threatened with extinction
to howl no more
across the frozen forests
of the world.
You came with friends to visit me,
a friend and no man's pet or creature,
accustomed to my human ways from birth
and loving how I speak and how I play,
my gentle hands
my quick responsive way
attuned to yours.

No fear between us — only that grave threat
unsensed by you
the teeming billions of my kind
extend to every creature on the earth;
well might we learn from you
the discipline, the tribal loyalty,
the rules that govern your proud race.
This planet will be poorer if wolves go
and none to howl across the deepening snow.

OLD WOLF

No savagery
in this abandonment: for weeks
a yearling from the pack had stayed nearby
through long night hunts, her scent
and slight familiar sounds
a comfort to the aging, grizzled wolf.

Near blind from cataracts
he sleeps away the nights
as well as days in Arctic solitude.
The hunts of youth
are earnest dreams, kaleidographed
in vivid golds behind his sightless eyes.

Awaking now
alone and cold and troubled
he howls at where the moon should be.
No answer from the pack.
He sleeps again,
a dreamless sleep this time.

WOLVES

I mourn much more, though I conceal the fact,
a wolf that dies than many of my own kind,
perhaps because I've known so few,
some six or seven in my time.
I've seen
nulliparous wolves
regurgitate their food to feed a pup
whose sire and dame were absent, heard
wolf music in the night.

Most men are ill at ease with wolves,
fearing what we cannot dominate.
Man grasps,
accrues
lays waste a planet
because he is afraid
of truth
of death
of wolves howling in the night.

RELUCTANT SAINT

A feathered bomb
rebounding from a crystal pane of glass
began my bondage. Unprepared
for such a desperate need
I gathered him, a junco, in my hand.

No prudent person would expect
such limp disordered feathers to
arrange themselves in flight again.
His plight was mine and I
his only chance. I made a nest
of twigs and paper, watched
him gently, stroked
his back and spoke
to him and o the litany —
the vows I made to a childhood god,
alone with a slate grey bird,
the promises I dare not break.

He flew and he was free
and I his bondsman here,
lest somewhere, some
accounting day
some junco fall beyond recall
beside some brittle pane of clear, clear glass,
and all
my fault.

MIGRATIONS

I hold the tiny warbler in my hand,
a yellowthroat. Were he a resident,
a finch or blue jay native to these parts,
he had not flown at such a break-neck speed
against the phantom forest in these panes.

Is not my life, small feathered friend, like yours
a series of migrations, constant trips
at promptings like the moon that moves the seas
one season to another — will it end
with mine a broken body, cold, inert,
held briefly by some stranger with warm hands,
bewildered, questioning and hurt?

PASSER MORTUUS EST

First day of winter —
in the grey belated dawn
a sparrow huddles motionless
inside the feeder shelter
and hardly stirs
when mourning doves arrive
until at length their bustling feeding rites
evict him and he flies.

I feel relief for he had seemed
hurt or maybe sick, his sloth
unnatural, foreboding.

I fill the feeders
an hour later, brushing off the snow
and turning, see the sparrow
on cold dry ground against the cellar wall.

Death is not far off.
He cringes, has no strength,
but minutes from the time he fled the doves,
to fly from me.

I think of paper nests
and warm rooms waiting
just beyond those walls, but know
that he will not survive the fright
of strange hands gathering, so I speak
then turn and leave him there,

and wonder, when it comes
if death might better be
a cat with fangs to quicken what must be
or a gently speaking giant with soft words
but powerless.

                        Midmorning.
I go outside again,
find him there
and lay him in a sheltered earthy place
beneath brown leaves.

POETS AND OTHER PEOPLE

The crows cawed incessantly this morning
    from some rendezvous

the other side of a stand of birch
    off Linekin Bay,

a gull scanned the water from his perch
    above the dock,

four sailing vessels moved stately, steadily
    through the channels —

all this under brilliant sun
    and flawless skies.

Poets and other people in the past have viewed
    as I do now

the settlement across this bay, the buildings
    unobtrusive, functional,

and longer still the cormorants, seals basking
    in the sun

on distant rocks, and heard these crows.

When I remember, and I often do, how much
    I love this planet,

this is the scene most often in my mind.
 I used to view myself

as middle man in a long line of lovers
 of this coast,

but lately I look with a terrible urgency,
 a sense not many more of us

will walk down to the water in the morning
 with our dogs

to watch the tide turn or listen
 to the crows.

One day last year at school we had a wolf
 and astronaut

to visit with our classes, help the children
 understand the times

we live in. The astronaut spoke knowingly
 of satellites and shuttles;

the wolf howled, and I could hear the scream
 of life betrayed,

and understand the legends of our race,
 the doomsday tales.

Forgive me if I seem too filled with doubts
and middle age.

The journals all are full of news this week,
none good, —

of shortages, of limited resources, governments
gone bad;

earnest, helpless men in conference and remedies
that fail.

It all seems interwoven, the patterns too complex
for us to know

what's caught up with us in this net. I've seen
tenacious life

at war with death in individuals, then seen
the systems fail.

I know how frail the stoutly beating heart
can be,

the strident lung. I think we have no charter
for our kind.

The instruments for self-destruction multiply,
these present will suffice.

For years I have accepted I shall die
as all men do.

What scalds my mind is knowing there may come
a day, and not far off,

when there are no poets or other people here
to hear these crows

all cawing in the morning, if indeed
a creature's left to caw,

to swim these waters, feel the wind, or watch
the sun come up.